RUNAWAYS
THE GOOD DIE YOUNG

Writer: **Brian K. Vaughan**

Penciler: **Adrian Alphona**

Inker: **Craig Yeung**

Colorist: **UDON's Christina Strain**

Letterer: **Virtual Calligraphy's Randy Gentile & Dave Sharpe**

Cover Artist: **Jo Chen**

Assistant Editor: **MacKenzie Cadenhead**

Editor: **C.B. Cebulski**

Runaways created by **Brian K. Vaughan & Adrian Alphona**

Collections Editor: **Jeff Youngquist**

Assistant Editor: **Jennifer Grünwald**

Book Designer: **Carrie Beadle**

Creative Director: **Tom Marvelli**

Sales Manager: **David Gabriel**

Editor in Chief: **Joe Quesada**

Publisher: **Dan Buckley**

PREVIOUSLY...

Teenager Alex Wilder and five other only children always though
that their parents were boring Los Angeles socialites, until th
kids witness the adults murder a young girl in some kind of dar
sacrificial ritual. The teens soon learn that their parents ar
partof a secret organization called The Pride, a collection o
crime bosses, time-traveling despots, alien overlords, ma
scientists, evil mutants, and dark wizards.

After stealing weapons and resources from these villainou
adults (including an encrypted book about The Pride, a mystica
decoder ring, and a psychic velociraptor named Old Lace), th
kids run away from home and vow to bring their parents t
justice. But with the help of operatives in the LAPD, The Prid
frames their children for the murder they committed, and th
fugitive Runaways are forced to retreat to a subterranea
hideout. Using the diverse powers and skills they inherited, th
kids now hope to atone for their parents' crimes by helpin
those in need.

But The Pride has other plans for their children...

#13

LAME!

It's been like a **week,** and there hasn't been **one** report of super heroes in L.A., much less anything about our psycho **parents** getting taken down!

Yeah, my clothes are starting to smell like **hideout.** I thought the Revengers were gonna **rescue** us!

Maybe Captain America and those guys are dealing with some kind of **space crisis** or whatever.

Or maybe those Cloak and Dagger tools we trusted **lied** to us. I bet they were working for our parents' goons in the LAPD all along.

We're just lucky "the man" is too stupid to find our--

I did it!

Did what, Alex? Finally got your 'fro under control?

Oh, wait, apparently not...

Listen, I finally deciphered the **Abstract!**

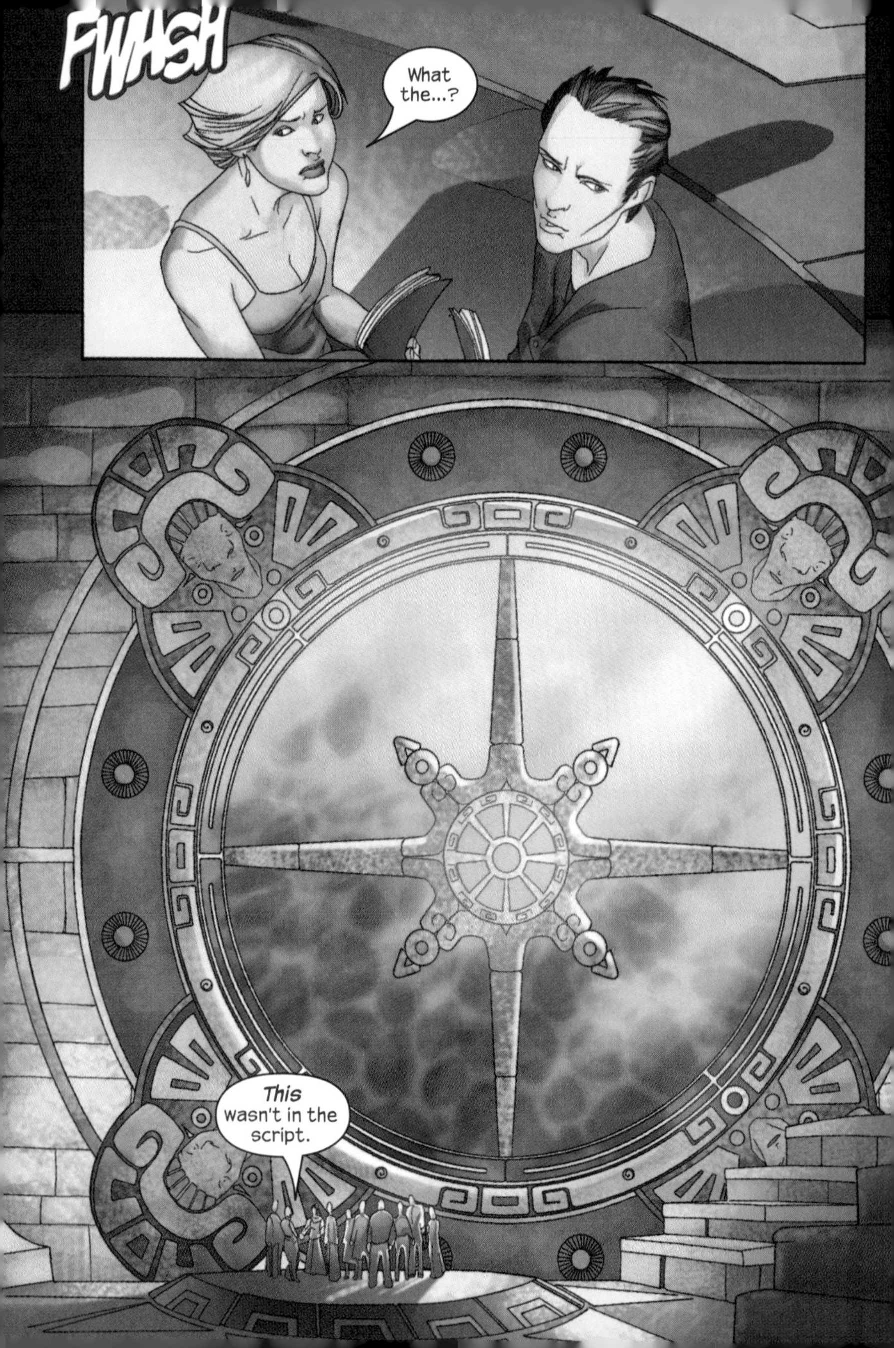
FWASH
What the...?
This wasn't in the script.

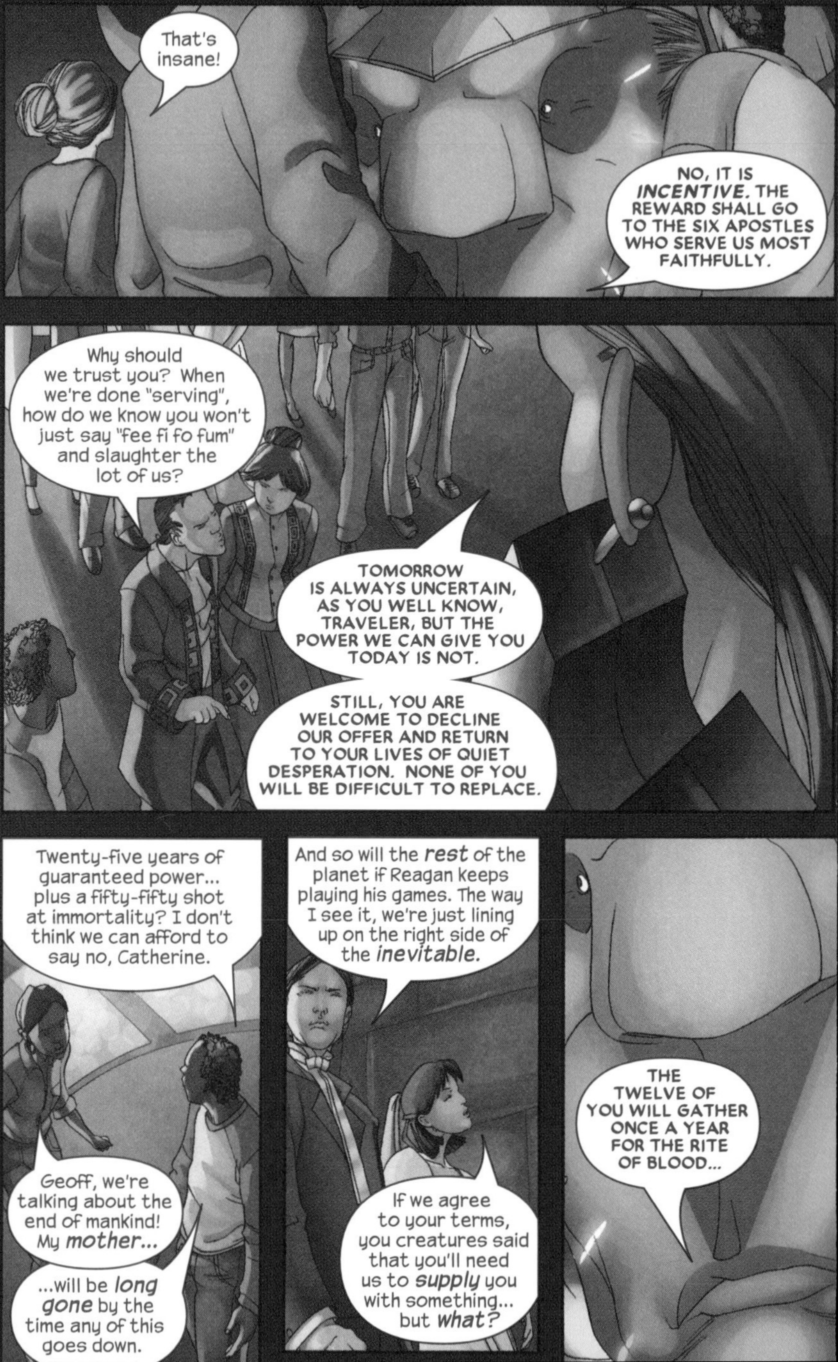

That's insane!

NO, IT IS **INCENTIVE.** THE REWARD SHALL GO TO THE SIX APOSTLES WHO SERVE US MOST FAITHFULLY.

Why should we trust you? When we're done "serving", how do we know you won't just say "fee fi fo fum" and slaughter the lot of us?

TOMORROW IS ALWAYS UNCERTAIN, AS YOU WELL KNOW, TRAVELER, BUT THE POWER WE CAN GIVE YOU TODAY IS NOT.

STILL, YOU ARE WELCOME TO DECLINE OUR OFFER AND RETURN TO YOUR LIVES OF QUIET DESPERATION. NONE OF YOU WILL BE DIFFICULT TO REPLACE.

Twenty-five years of guaranteed power... plus a fifty-fifty shot at immortality? I don't think we can afford to say no, Catherine.

And so will the *rest* of the planet if Reagan keeps playing his games. The way I see it, we're just lining up on the right side of the *inevitable.*

THE TWELVE OF YOU WILL GATHER ONCE A YEAR FOR THE RITE OF BLOOD...

Geoff, we're talking about the end of mankind! My *mother*...

...will be *long gone* by the time any of this goes down.

If we agree to your terms, you creatures said that you'll need us to *supply* you with something... but *what*?

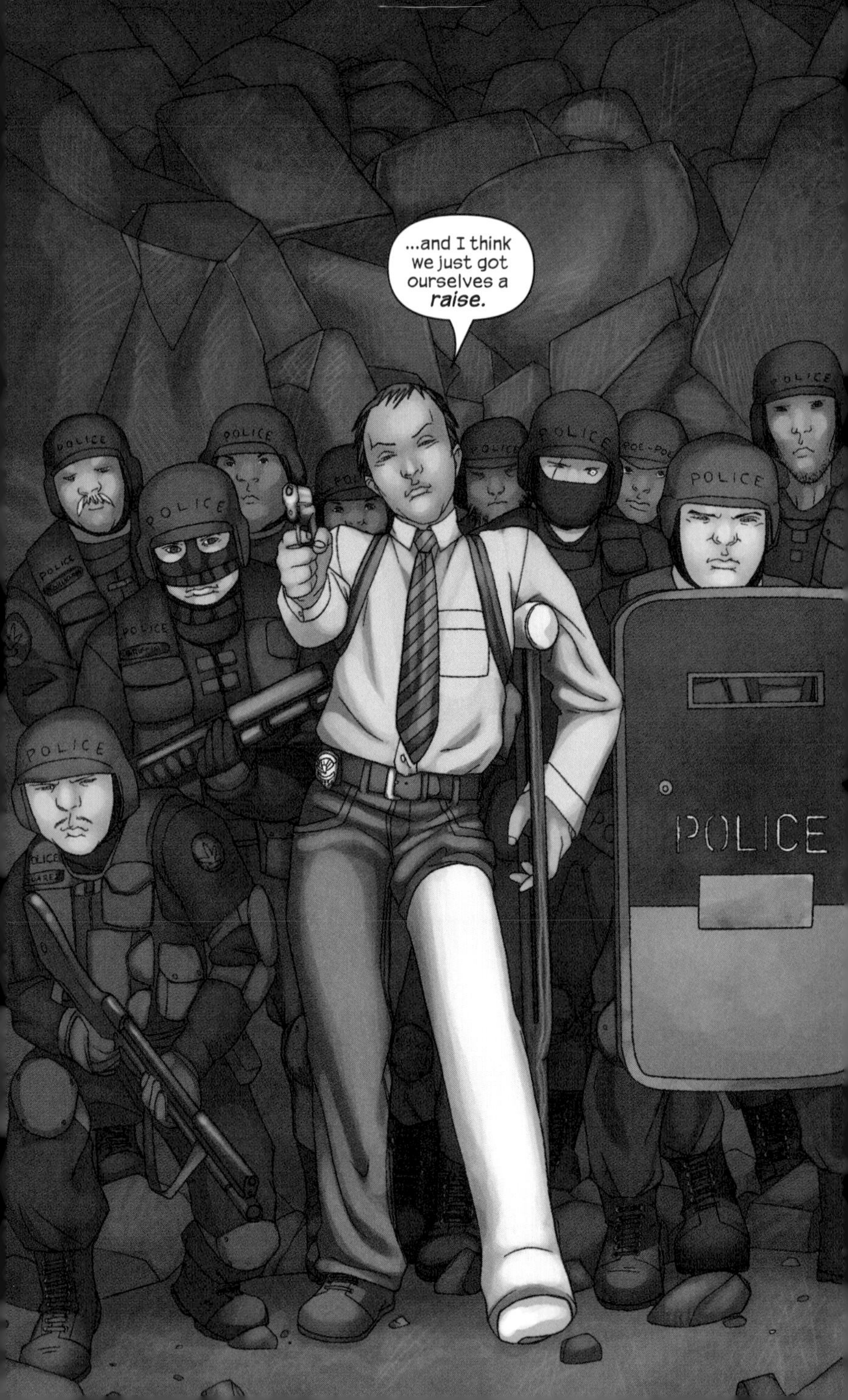
...and I think we just got ourselves a *raise.*
POLICE

#14

The Wilder Residence
Los Angeles, California
4:33 P.M.
Mr. Wilder?

The twelve of us joined The Pride because we each wanted one of the Gibborim's six tickets to paradise for *ourselves.*
We *never* would have given up that shot at eternal life if my wife hadn't become *pregnant...* if *all* of us hadn't decided that we needed *little ones* to share our empty mansions with.
But it was *years* ago that we agreed to donate our chance at immortality to those six kids. Back then, none of us imagined that we would ever *want* to live forever.
Surviving to an age like *forty* sounded like an eternity already, more than enough time to enjoy all the Gibborim had granted us.
But now we're *old men,* rapidly approaching the Final Wave, and the ungrateful brats we sacrificed everything for have *abandoned* us.
Admit it, some nights, you think about *letting* your son perish with the rest of this wretched populace... and taking his spot in the Next World for *yourself.*
NEVER!
hkk

I have done *terrible* things in my life, but for the last sixteen years, I have been confident that I was doing them for a *noble* reason.

I am going to find Alex and give him what is rightfully his, and I will *destroy* anyone who stands in my way.

...thank... you.

What did you say?

Thank you... for saying what wanted to hear. My son an I have had our difference but I love Chase more than life itself. *Literally.*

My wife and I feel the exact same way that you do, but I needed to be *certain* that we were all on the same page.

ou were .esting me?

Geoffrey, be rational. We're a group of thieves and... and *murderers.* I've never trusted *any* of--

Stand by... my wife programmed our chronometers to scan police radios for certain *key phrases.*

Apparently, a patrolman just received an anonymous tip about a white van like my *son's* parked in Bronson

Then we have to move *now*... before one of our overzealous agents decides to take matters into his *own*

DEET DEET

"The Hostel"
Bronson Canyon,
California
5:22 P.M.
Your folks are gonna *love* this.
No way!
You tools can't even find ***Saddam...*** but you found ***us?***

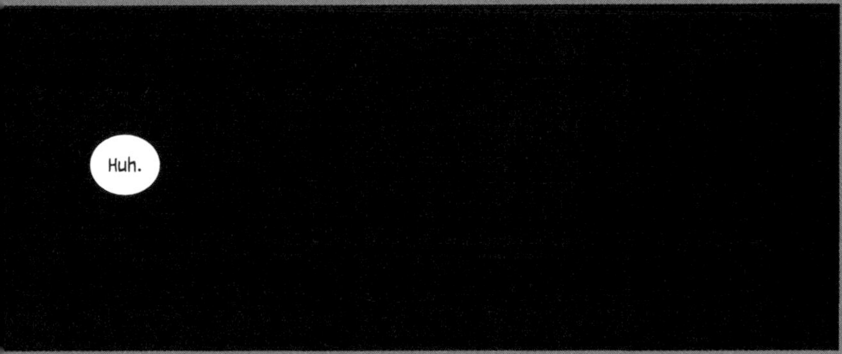
Huh.

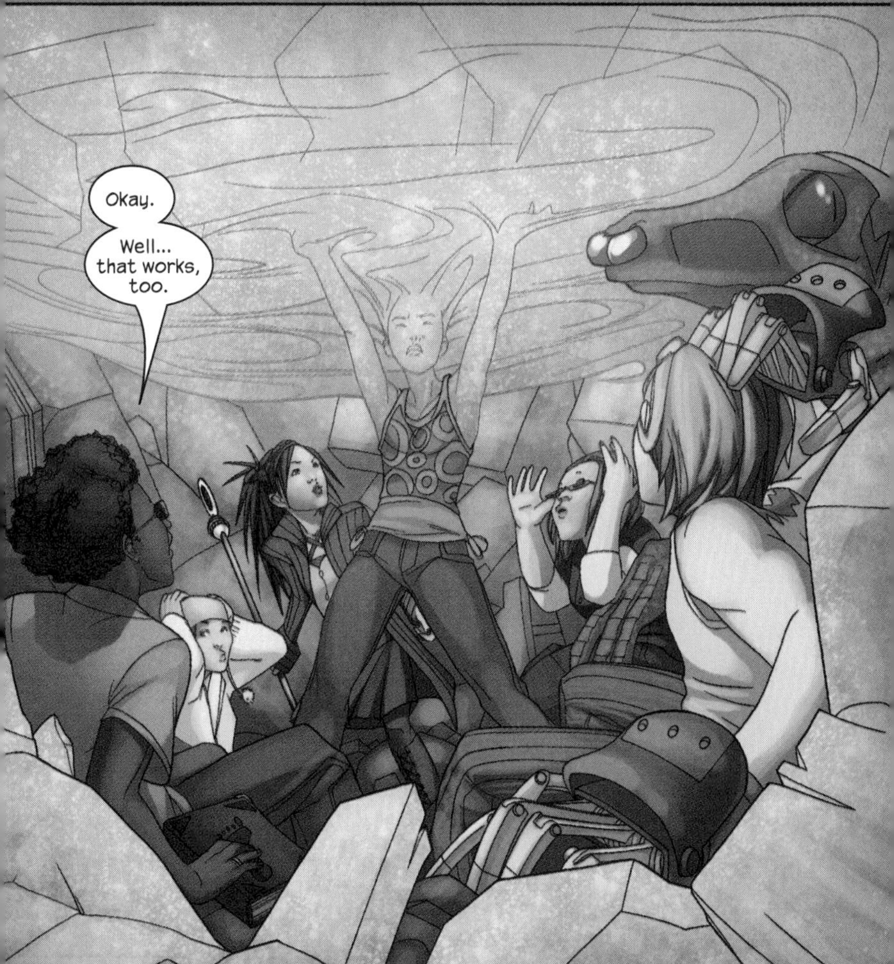
Okay.
Well... that works, too.

Is she *still* asleep?

What do you think, Talkback?

Molly practically dug us all the way to *China.*

I wish. We covered some good ground tonight...

...but not *enough.*

Are you *blind*, boss? Let's just build a new base *here*!

I don't think so, Dr. Evil. This place may be fenced off, but in a few hours, it'll be crawling with security guards looking for teens who are making out... and/or on the run from the *law*.

Then what are we *supposed* to do? The Avengers never showed up to help us, and it's pretty freakin' obvious we can't go to the *cops*.

As long as our 'rents are running Los Angeles, we gotta stay on the downlow!

Unless we take care of The Pride *ourselves*.

All *twelve* of them?

Nico, we barely lived through a fight against *three* of our parents.

That was months ago, Karolina... before we survived a bunch of vampires, two super heroes, and an entire S.W.A.T. team.

Yeah, survived... not *defeated*.

Says who? We've got our parents' *playbook*... and a coach who knows how to *read* it.

We're definitely better than we used to be, but we don't have what it takes to win the game yet.

Listen, we can use the Abstract to figure out the next time our parents are gonna be preoccupied with something else.
We'll hit them when they're least expecting it!
But what about what that detective said... about one of us secretly working for The Pride?
Yeah, how do we know we're not being led into some sort of trap?
You think I'm the traitor?
Leave her alone, Gert.
How come you keep sticking up for Nico, Alex? She totaled our crib! Or maybe you two are both rats...?
Guys, settle!
Don't you get it? That cop probably wanted to divide us. If we keep fighting like this, we're playing right into the hands of the bad guys.
Okay, I say Karolina's the mole.
Seconded.

#15

Thirty Feet Beneath Los Angeles
7:58 P.M.
If it wasn't for the smell...
...this would sorta be *awesome.*

Uh-oh, this is usually when I start to fall asleep...
You said you wanted to sit at the big kids' table, right, Molly? If you're really going to help us, you have to listen to Alex.
The Rite of Thunder is a ceremony where all twelve of our parents take the spirit they captured at the Rite of Blood... and feed it to those evil Gibborim guys they work for.
The Rite of Blood... that's the one where we saw that chick get stabbed to death, right?
Our parents murdered that girl. We can't just let some giant monsters eat her soul, too.
Whoa, hold on, I'm an agnostic. I'm sorry, but I'm not going to risk my life trying to rescue something I'm not even sure I believe in!
This is about more than theology, Gert. These souls are supposedly what give the Gibborim the power they'll need to someday destroy the whole planet.
Besides, our folks only appear before the Gibborim once a year, and when they do, they're supposed to enter "humbly", which I think translates to "without weapons".
Sweet, that means we'd have a slight edge on them. Sounds like the perfect time for a full-court press. How long do we have before the next one of these Thunderdome things?
About four hours.

Maybe I should have mentioned this earlier, but shouldn't we be concerned about the *bends?*
I mean, we came really far down really fast.
Nah, I took *scuba* last summer. The bends only happen when you go *up* too quickly.
Besides, my staff automatically regulated our pressure.
I've finally figured out how to make this thing look out for us.

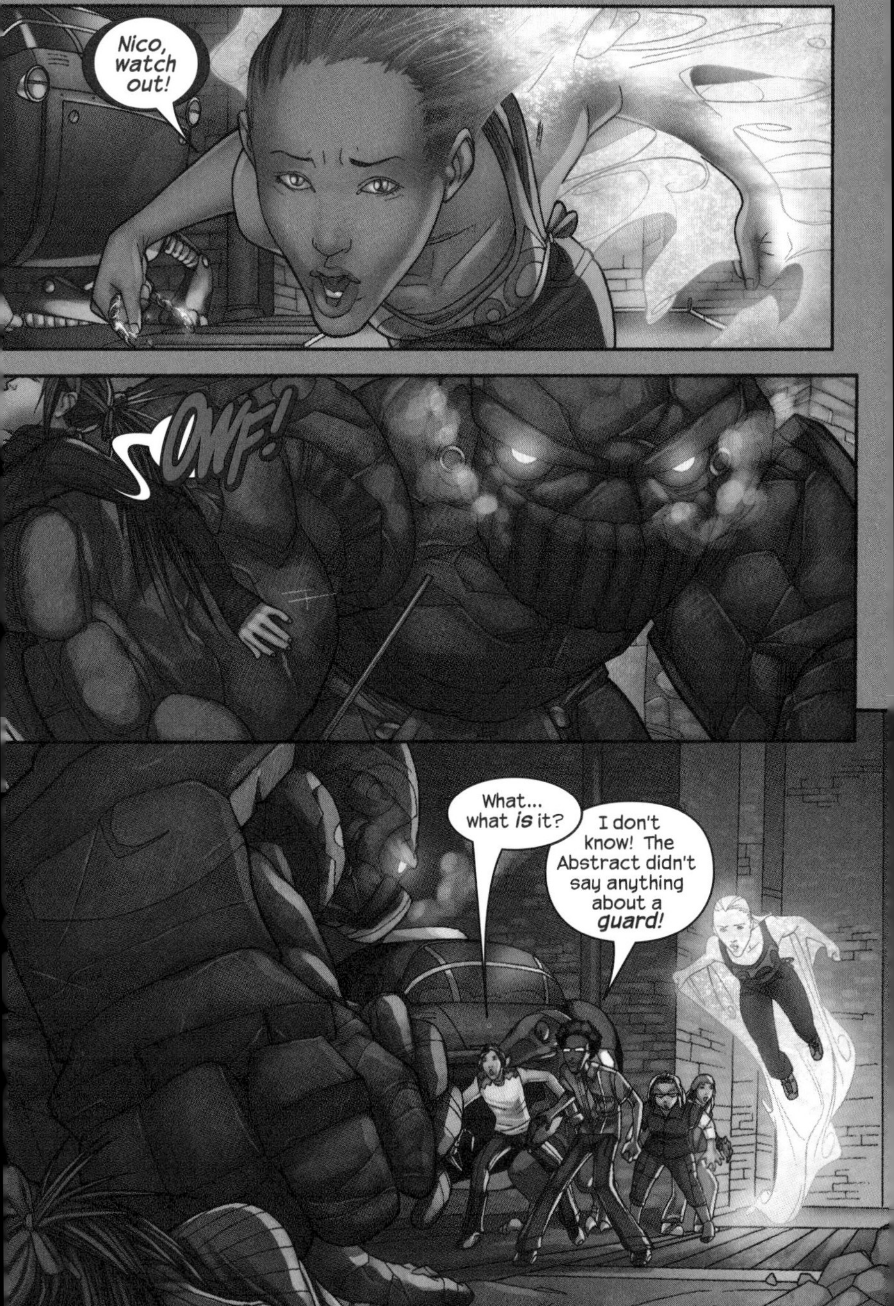
Nico, watch out!
OWF!
What... what *is* it?
I don't know! The Abstract didn't say anything about a *guard!*

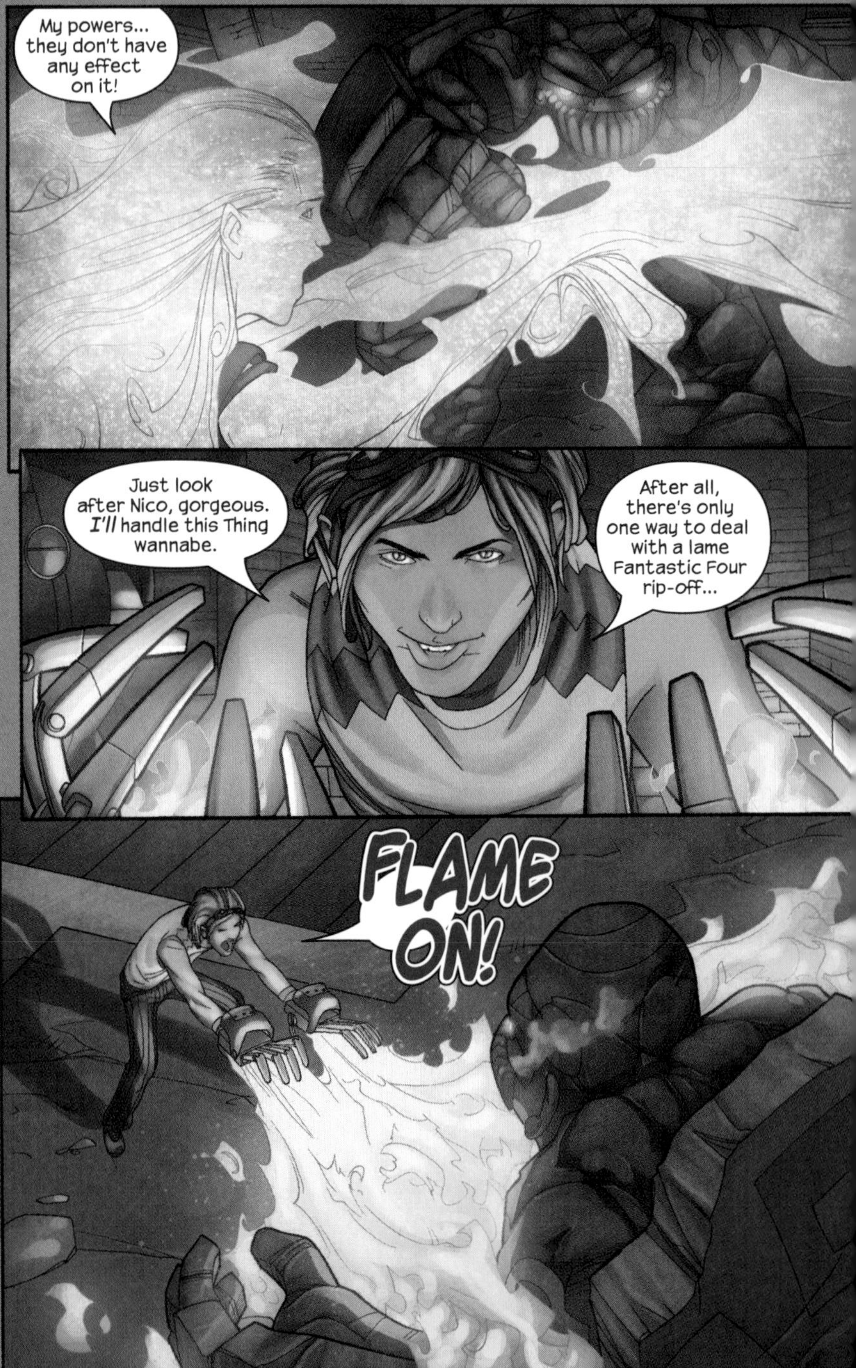
My powers... they don't have any effect on it!
Just look after Nico, gorgeous. *I'll* handle this Thing wannabe.
After all, there's only one way to deal with a lame Fantastic Four rip-off...
FLAME ON!

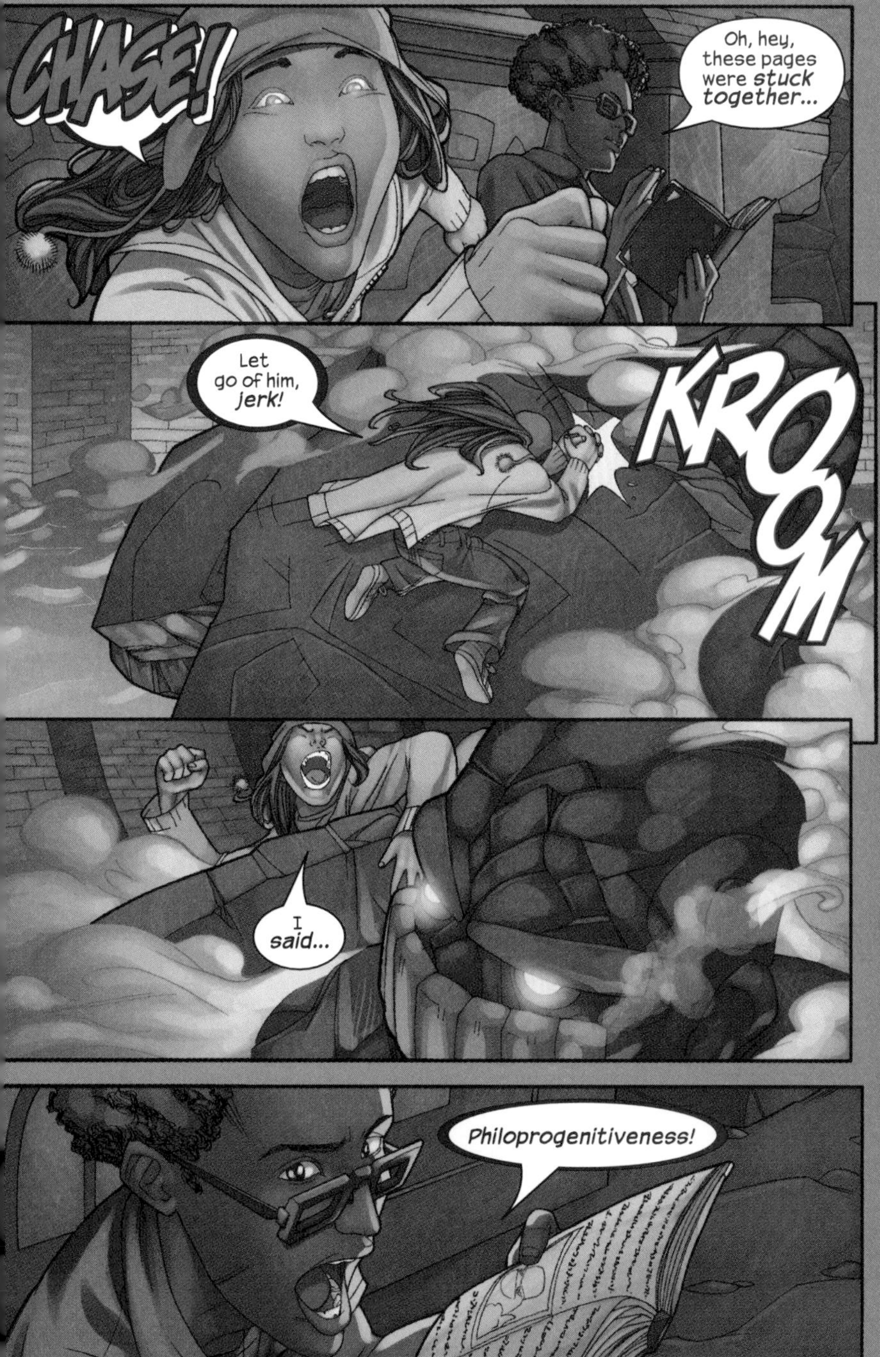
CHASE!
Oh, hey, these pages were stuck together...
Let go of him, jerk!
KROOM
I said...
Philoprogenitiveness!

#16

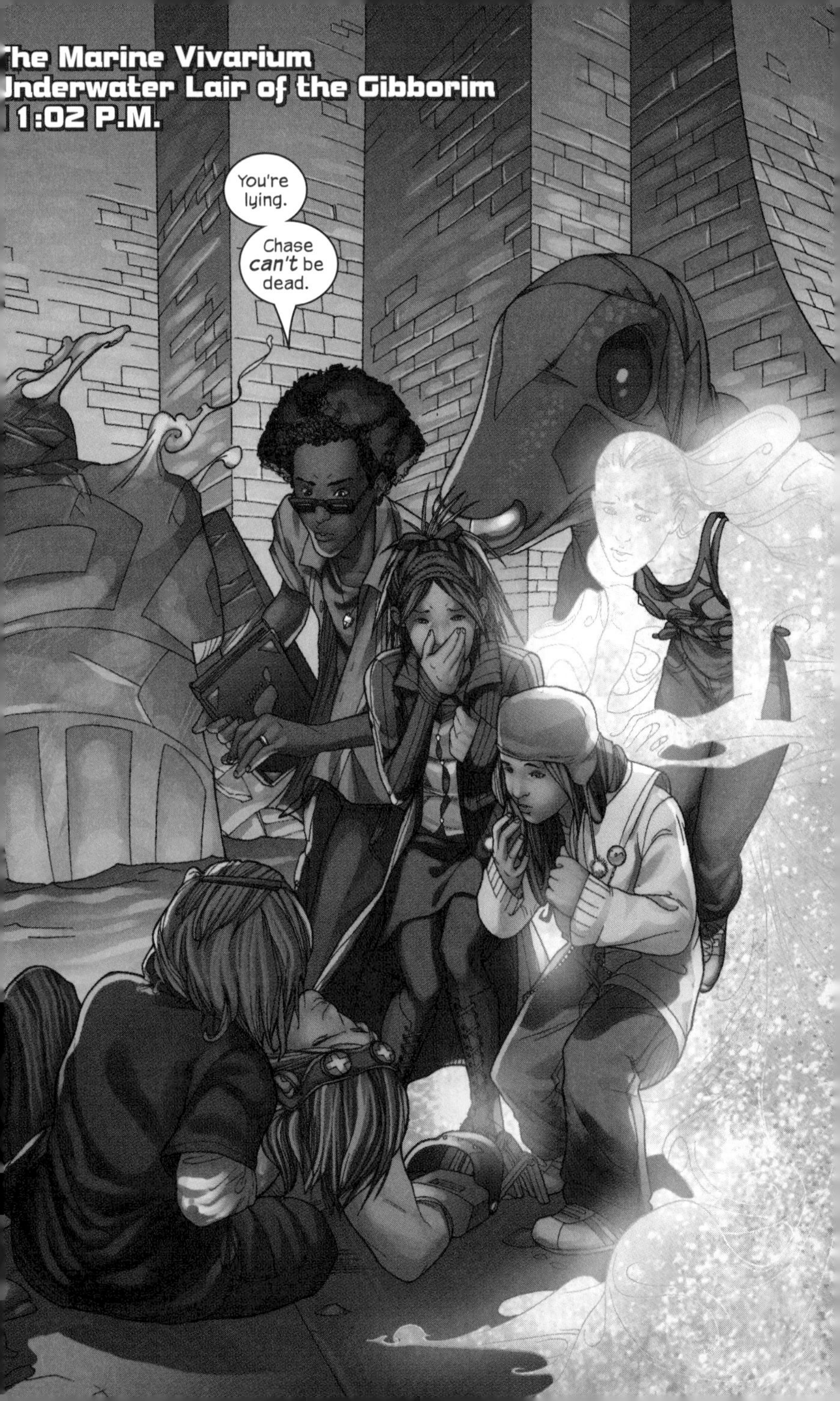

The Marine Vivarium
Underwater Lair of the Gibborim
1:02 P.M.
You're lying.
Chase can't be dead.

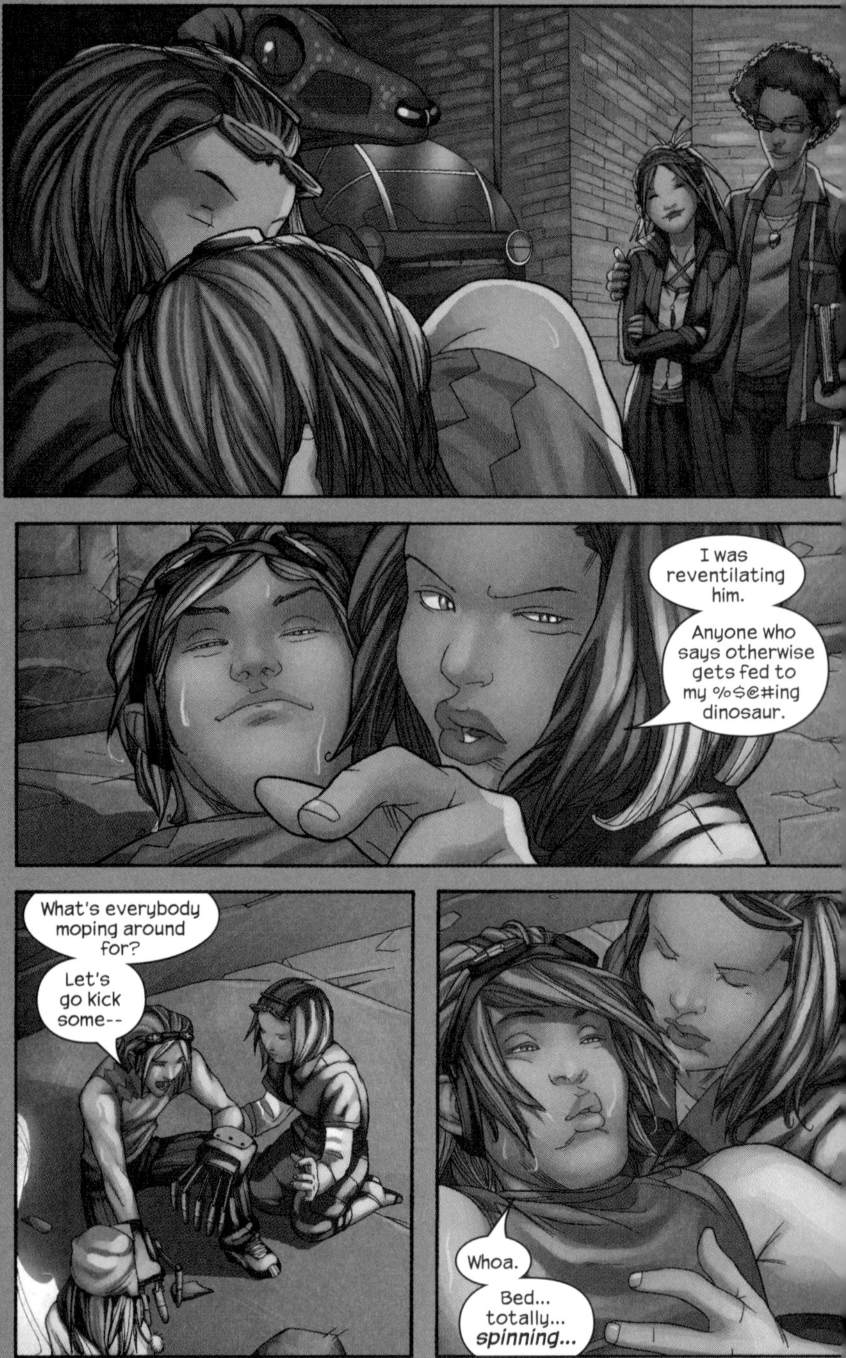
I was reventilating him.
Anyone who says otherwise gets fed to my %$@#ing dinosaur.
What's everybody moping around for?
Let's go kick some--
Whoa.
Bed... totally... *spinning...*

Do you ever have second thoughts, Stacey?
Since when is the "dark sorcerer" uncomfortable with a little black magic?
It's not just the Rite of Thunder. My heart hardened to these unholy ceremonies years ago. I'm talking about what they're meant to accomplish.
Are you still willing to help destroy the entire planet?
Oh, heavens, yes. Before my dolt of a husband totaled our 4-D portico permanently, we visited thousands of possible futures, each worse than the last.
And all of these timelines were overrun with the same wretched thing: super heroes.
The X-Men, the Avengers, the Fantastic bloody Four... their kind dominated every era, ensuring that people like us never challenged the mundane status quo.
Believe me, a world filled with fifty-year-old men punching one another is no place for children.
The next generation deserves something new... and that's exactly what we're going to give them.

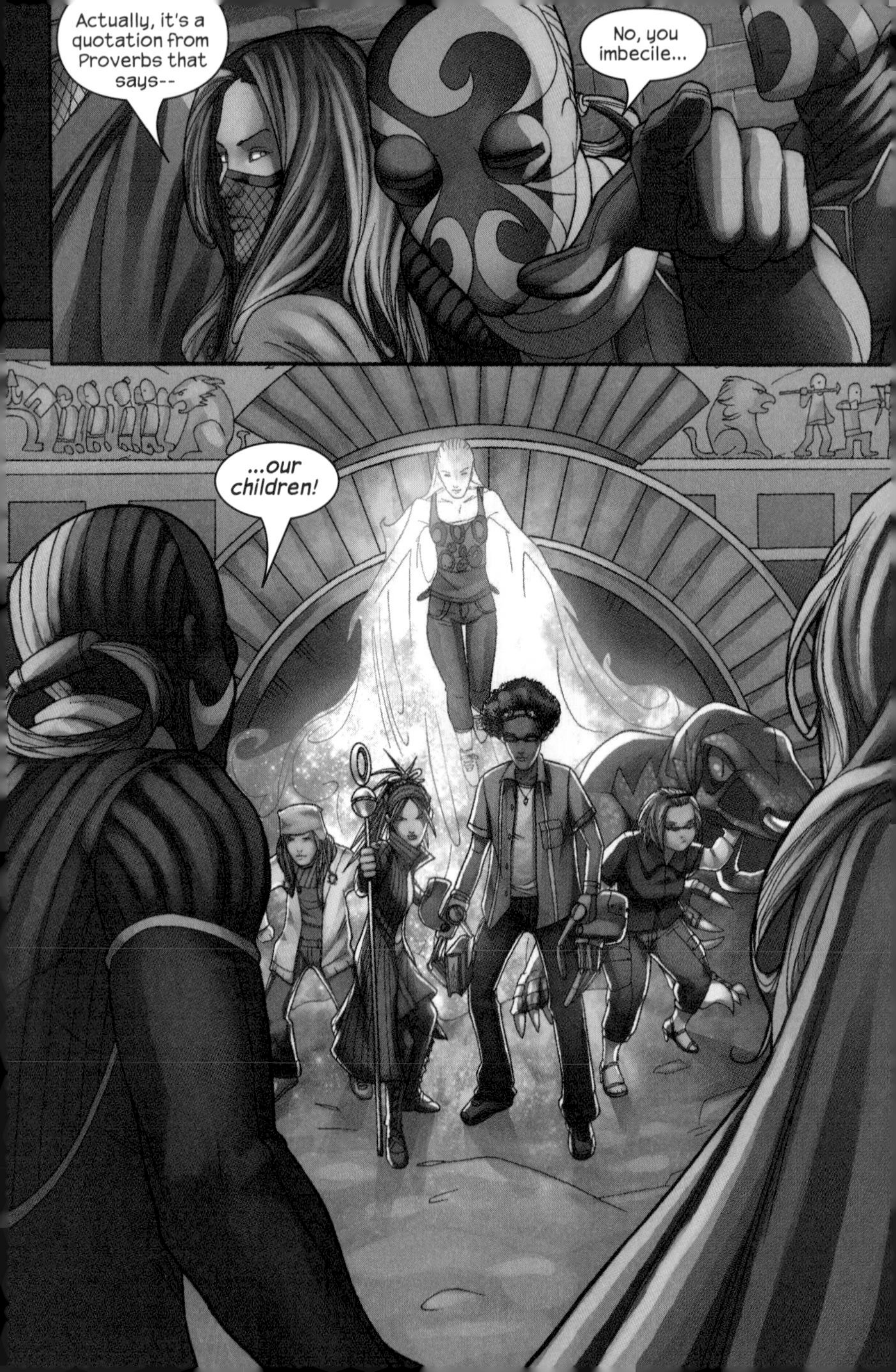
Actually, it's a quotation from Proverbs that says--
No, you imbecile...
...our children!

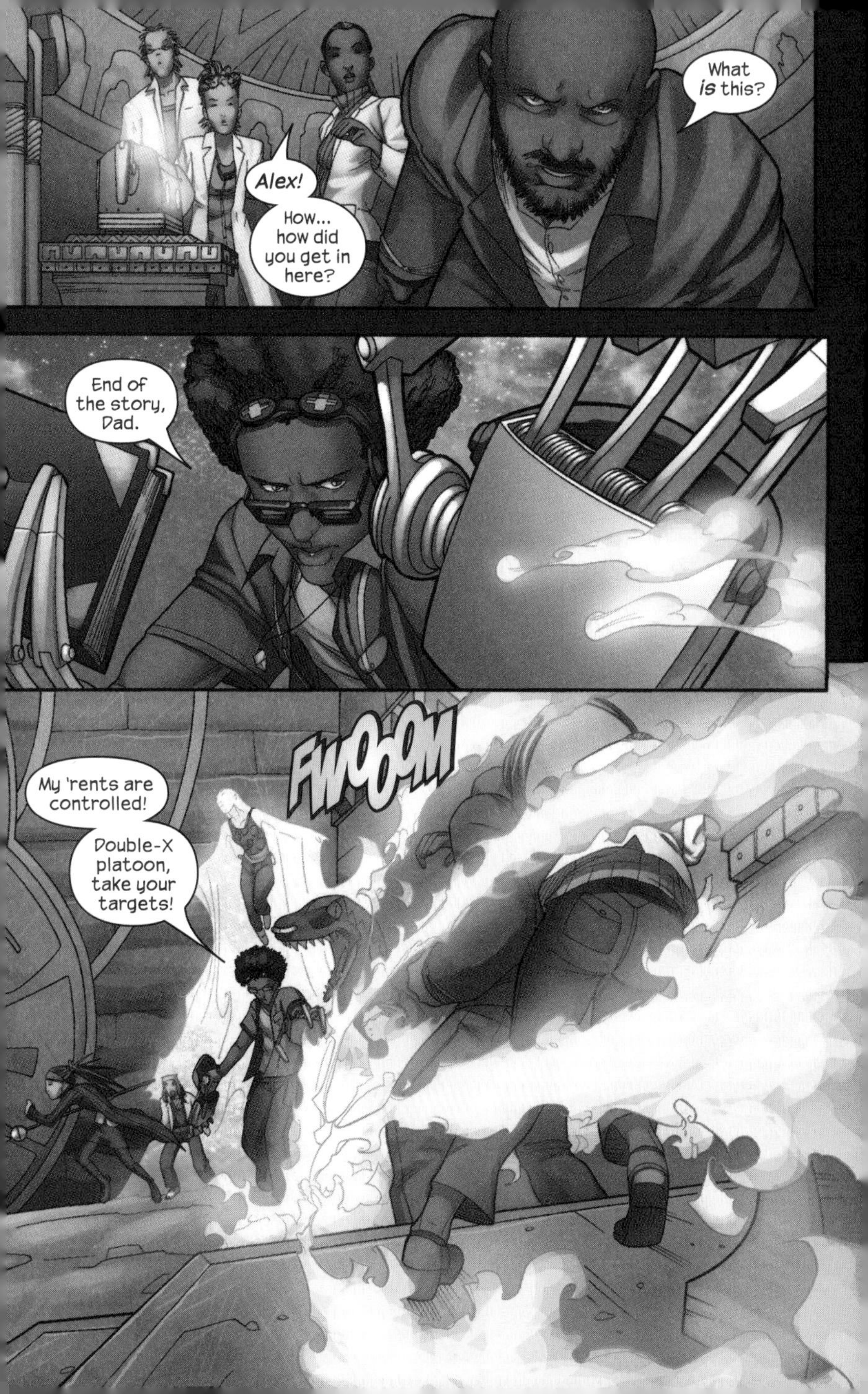
What *is* this?
Alex!
How... how did you get in here?
End of the story, Dad.
FWOOOM
My 'rents are controlled!
Double-X platoon, take your targets!

Remember the plan, girl.

If anything happens to me, you take your marching orders from *Alex*.

Lovely to see you again, Gertrude... but I believe we've been through this routine before.

Your little pet is physically *incapable* of harming your dear old mum and me.

Be cool, babe.

You *know* our family's powers don't work on each other, Karolina.

Ready?

Set.

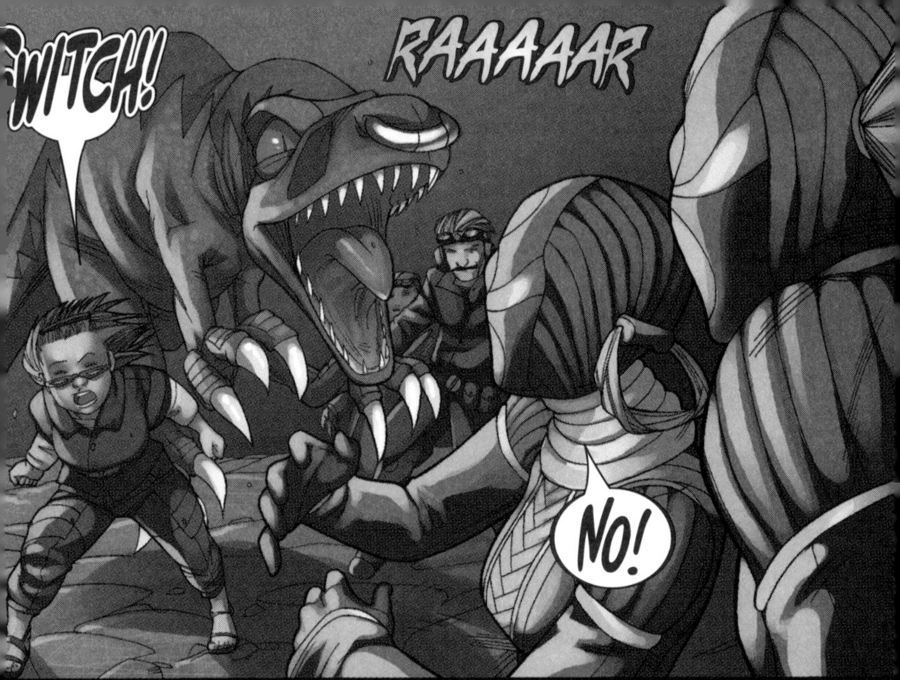
SWITCH!
RAAAAAR
NO!

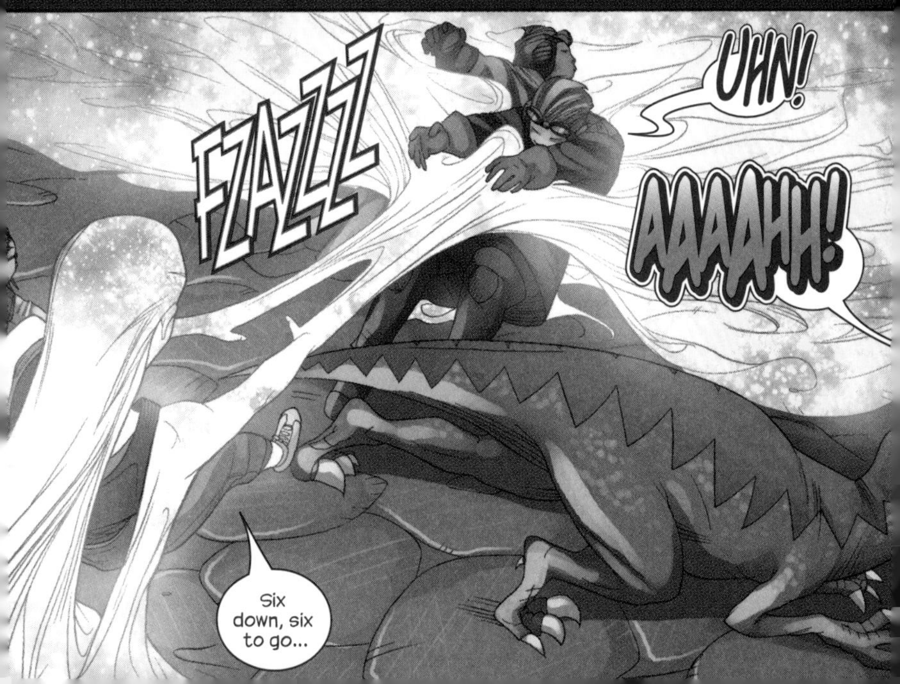
FZAZZZ
UHN!
AAAAHH!
Six down, six to go...

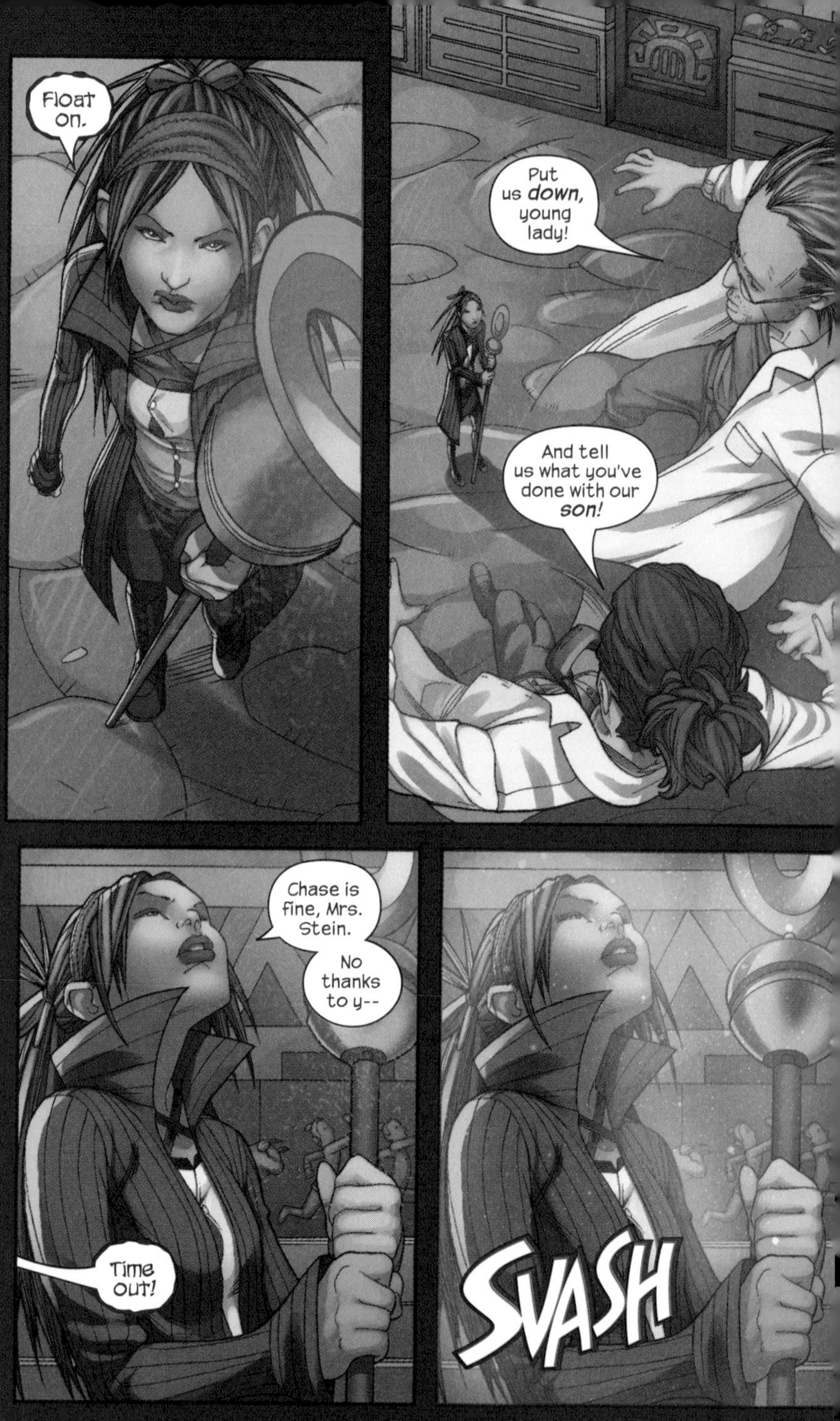
Float on.
Put us *down,* young lady!
And tell us what you've done with our *son!*
Chase is fine, Mrs. Stein.
No thanks to y--
Time out!
SVASH

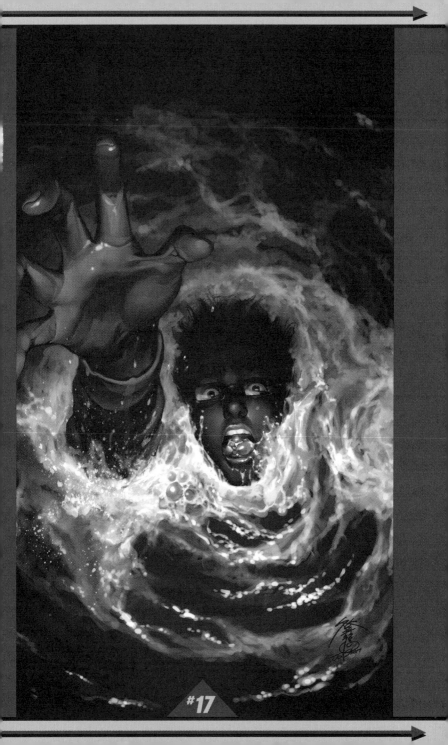

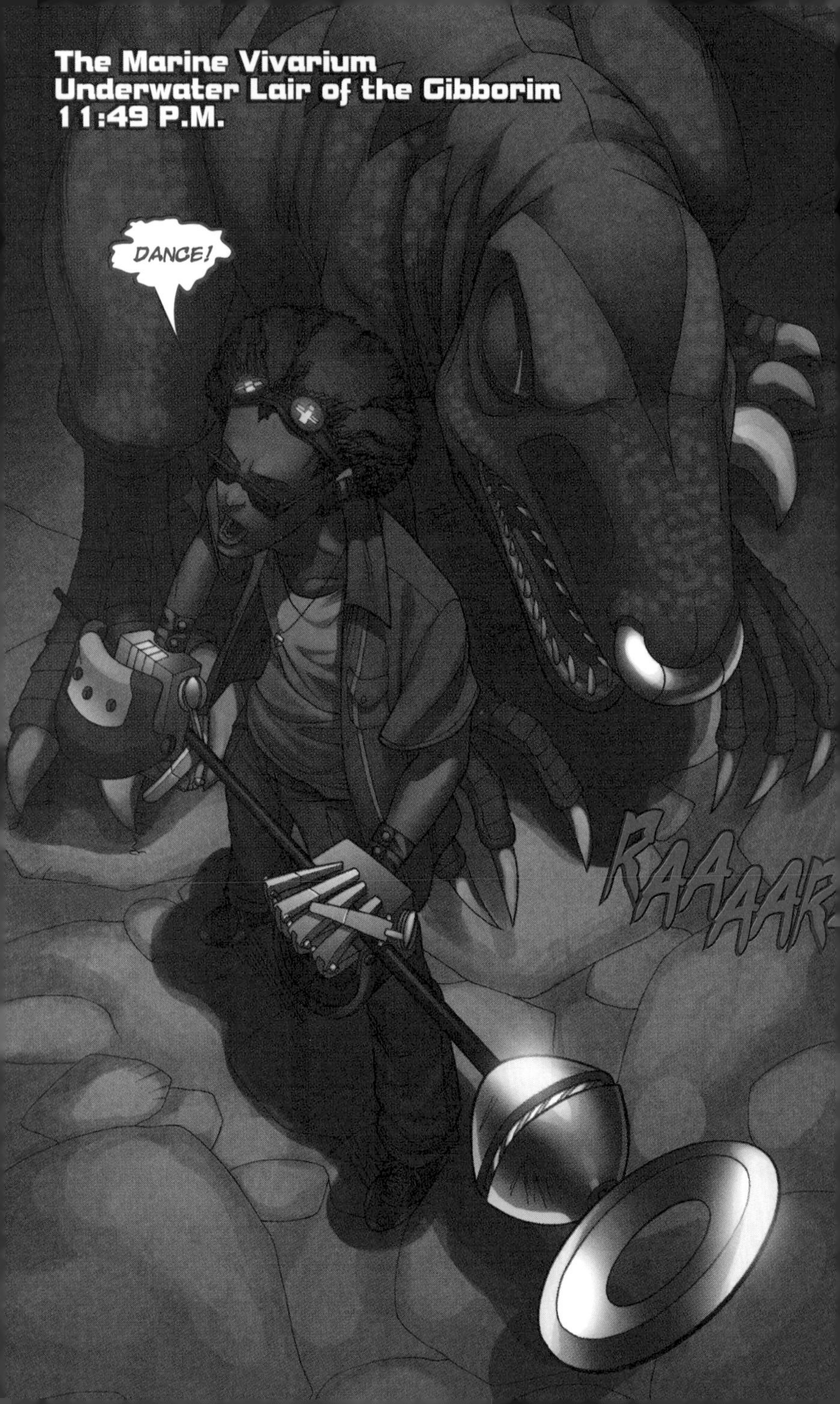
The Marine Vivarium
Underwater Lair of the Gibborim
11:49 P.M.
DANCE!
RAAAAR

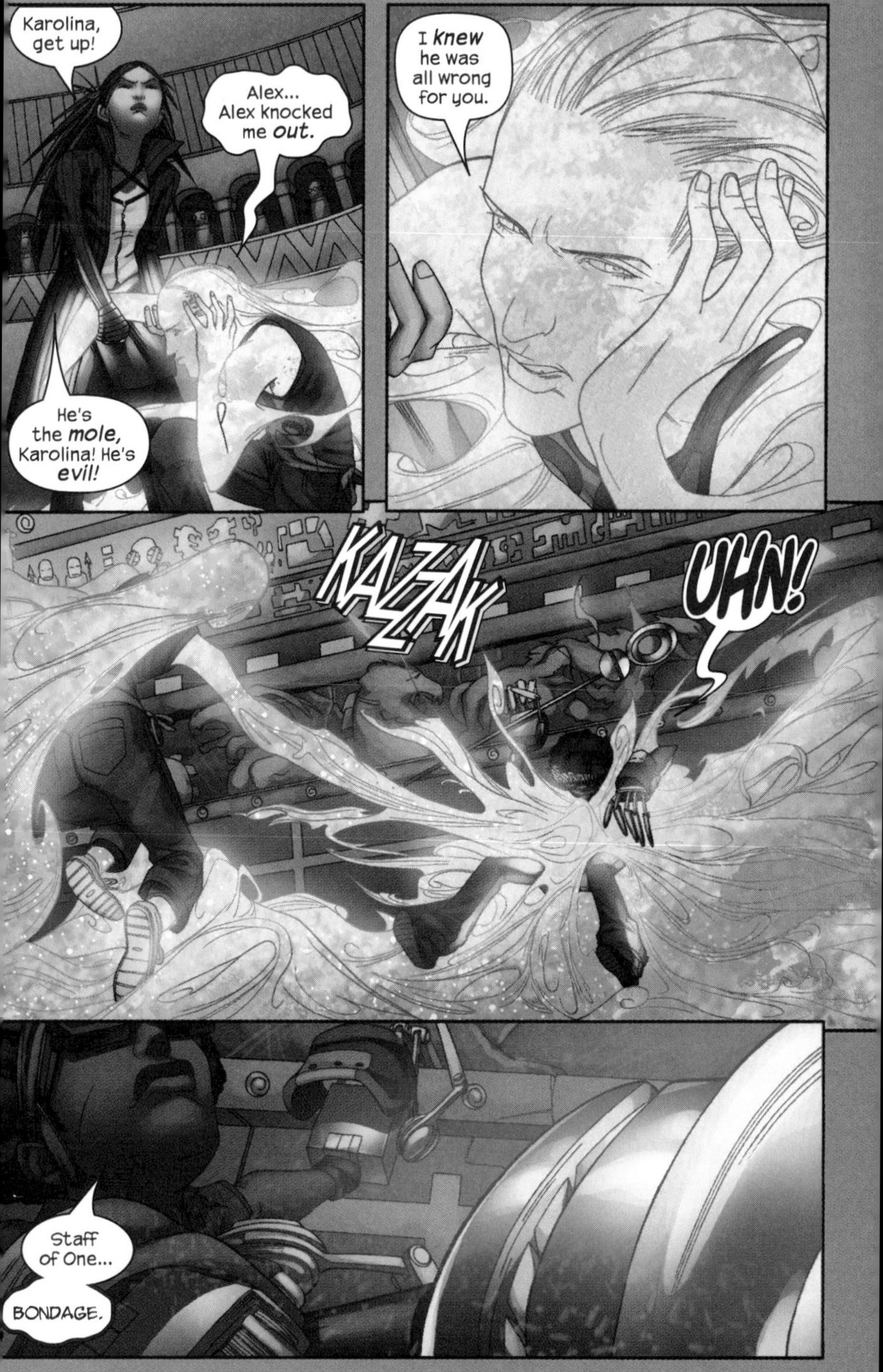
Karolina, get up!
Alex... Alex knocked me out.
He's the mole, Karolina! He's evil!
I knew he was all wrong for you.
KAZZAK
UHN!
Staff of One...
BONDAGE.

You're *lying.*
That's... that's ***all*** you do.
Her mom and dad were plotting to execute mine.
Sins of the father, right?
Please! I... I don't want to die anymore! I don't want to--
KROOOM

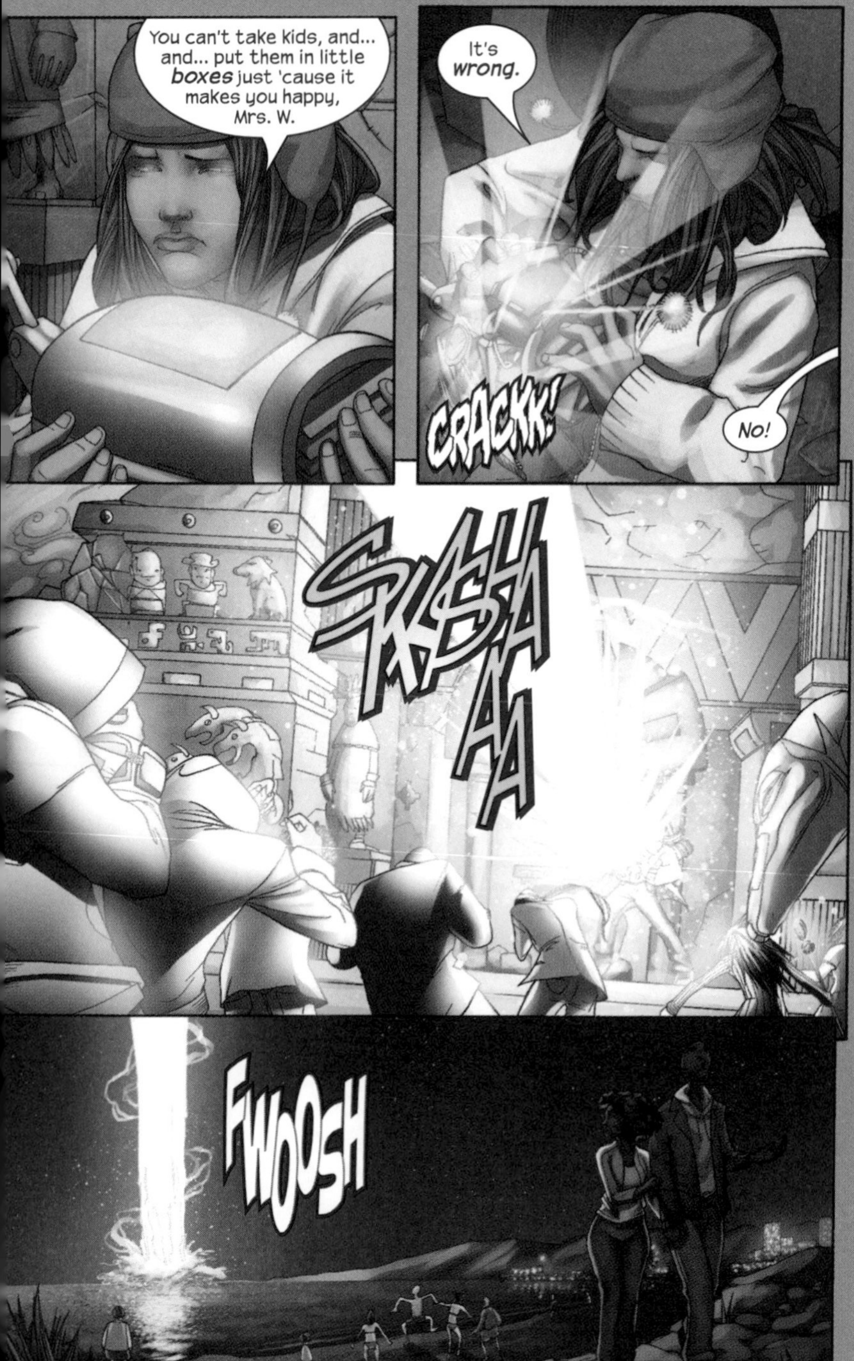
You can't take kids, and... and... put them in little **boxes** just 'cause it makes you happy, Mrs. W.
It's ***wrong.***
CRACKK!
No!
SKASHAAA
FWOOSH

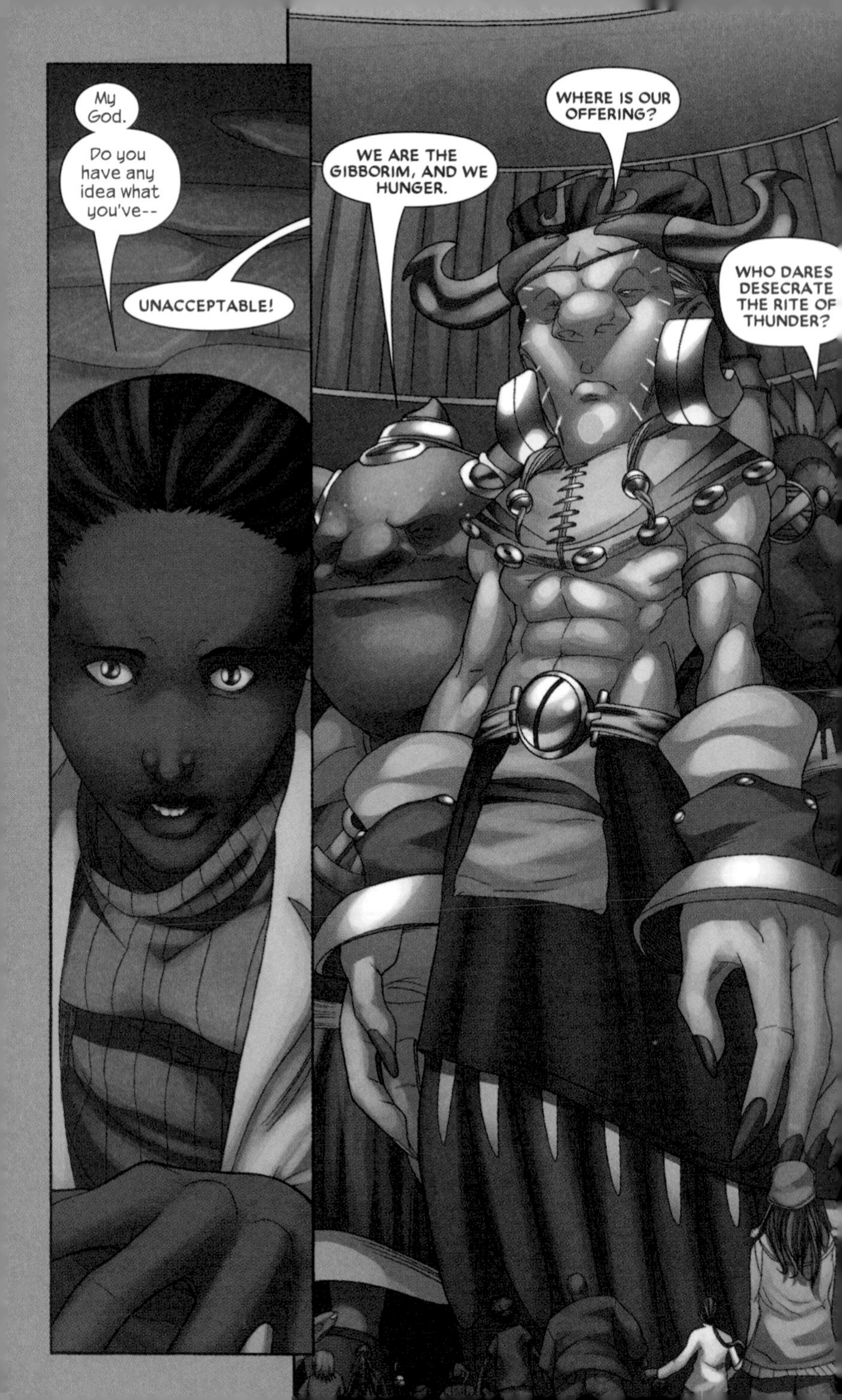
My God.
Do you have any idea what you've--
UNACCEPTABLE!
WE ARE THE GIBBORIM, AND WE HUNGER.
WHERE IS OUR OFFERING?
WHO DARES DESECRATE THE RITE OF THUNDER?

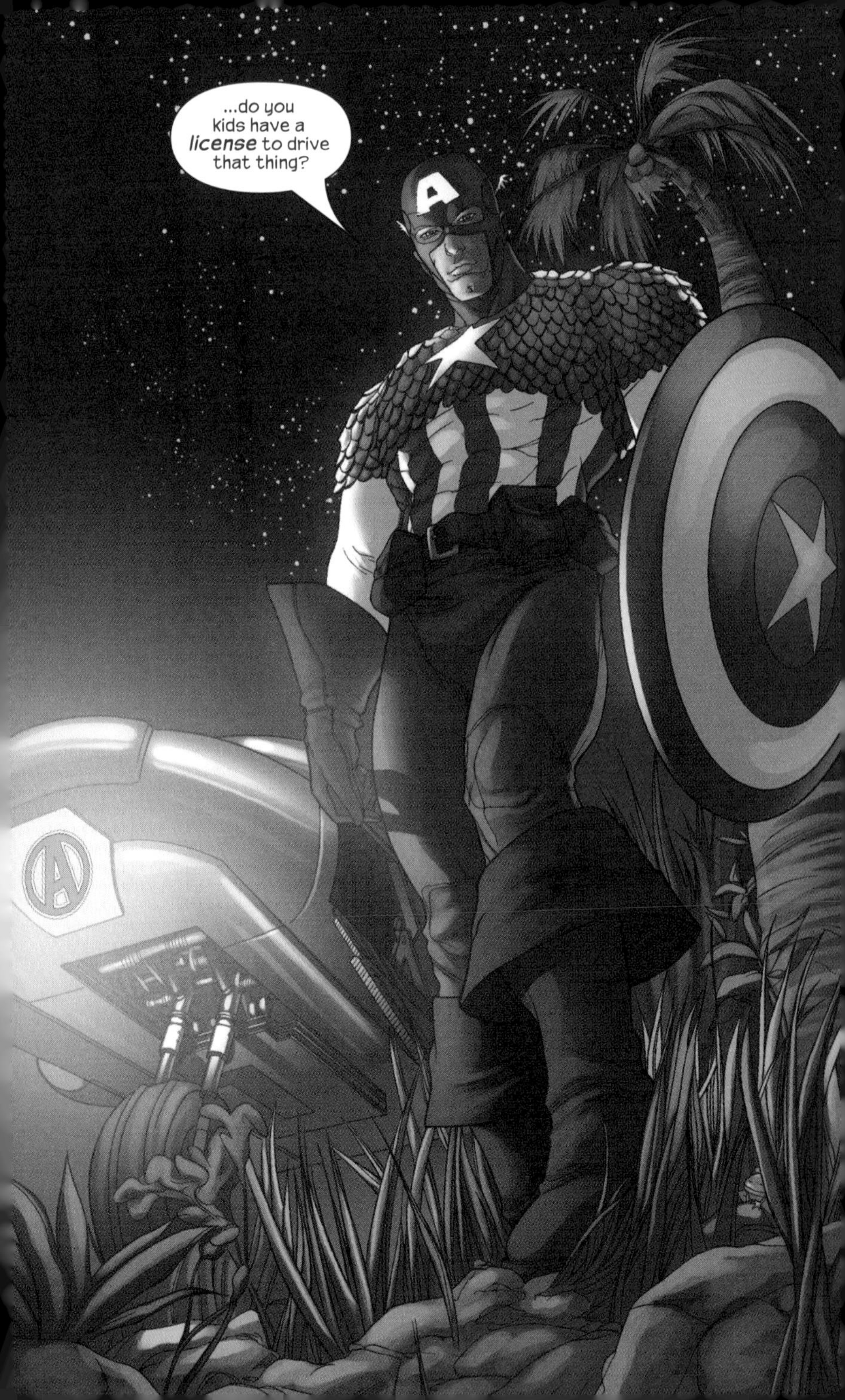
...do you kids have a *license* to drive that thing?

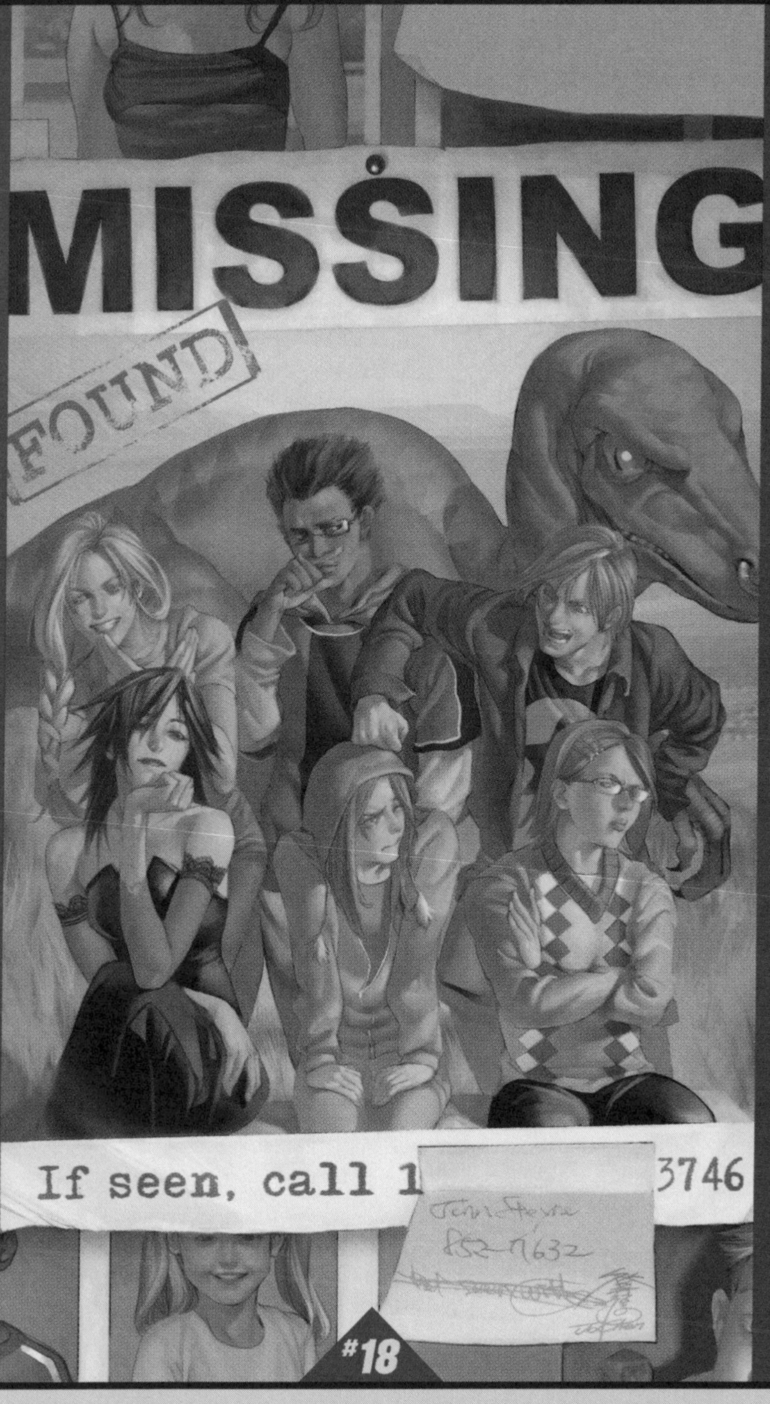
MISSING
FOUND
If seen, call 1
3746

#18

I'm Chester Biloxi, and that's the question six area teenagers recently had to ask themselves... and it's what we'll be talking about today on "Tsunami", Los Angeles' most *exciting* news magazine.

As we all know, three months ago, it was revealed that twelve of our city's most prominent socialites were actually part of a villainous secret organization known as *The Pride.*

According to documents obtained by New York-based super-group *The Avengers,* these seemingly normal families had criminal operatives placed throughout business, government, and perhaps most disturbingly, *law enforcement* here in California.

Though The Pride's true agenda remains a mystery, an exhaustive federal investigation has seen scores of corporate CEOs, high-ranking politicians, and even police officers indicted on charges ranging from racketeering to *homicide.*

And while the Avengers have been instrumental in aiding in the systematic dismantlement of this shadowy cabal's far-reaching network of conspirators, they are *not* responsible for the defeat of The Pride themselves.

That honor apparently goes to the six only *children* of these murderous adults, who ran away from home after witnessing their parents *kill* a young girl in some kind of occult ceremony.

In the hopes of learning more about this amazing story, our own Cadie MacDunnough recently caught up with *Captain America* outside of City Hall.

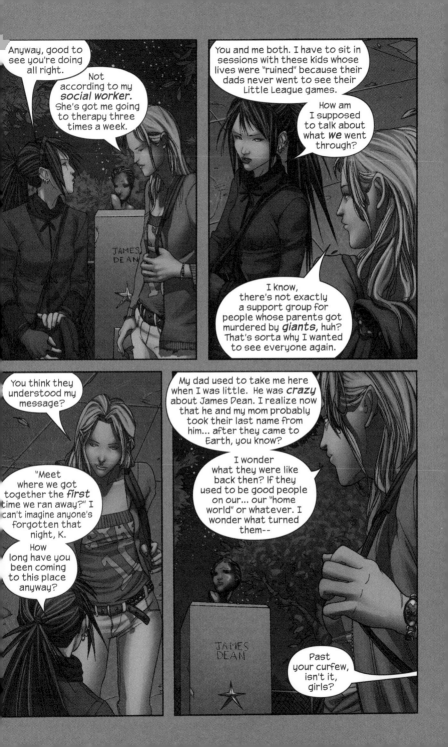

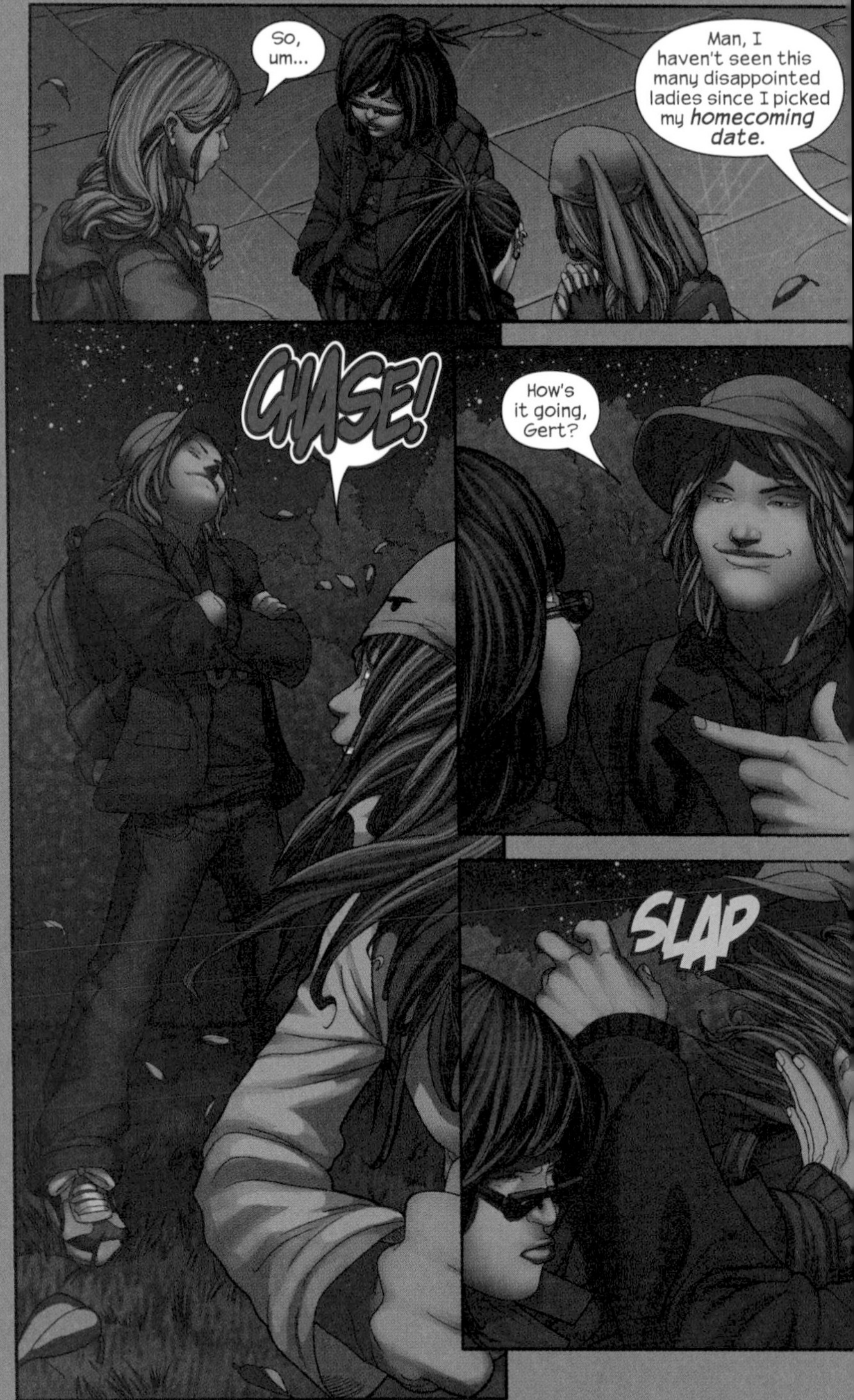

So, um...
Man, I haven't seen this many disappointed ladies since I picked my *homecoming date.*
CHASE!
How's it going, Gert?
SLAP

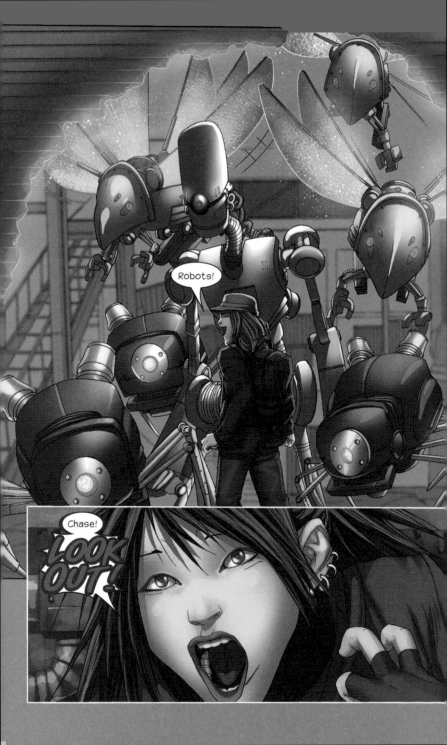

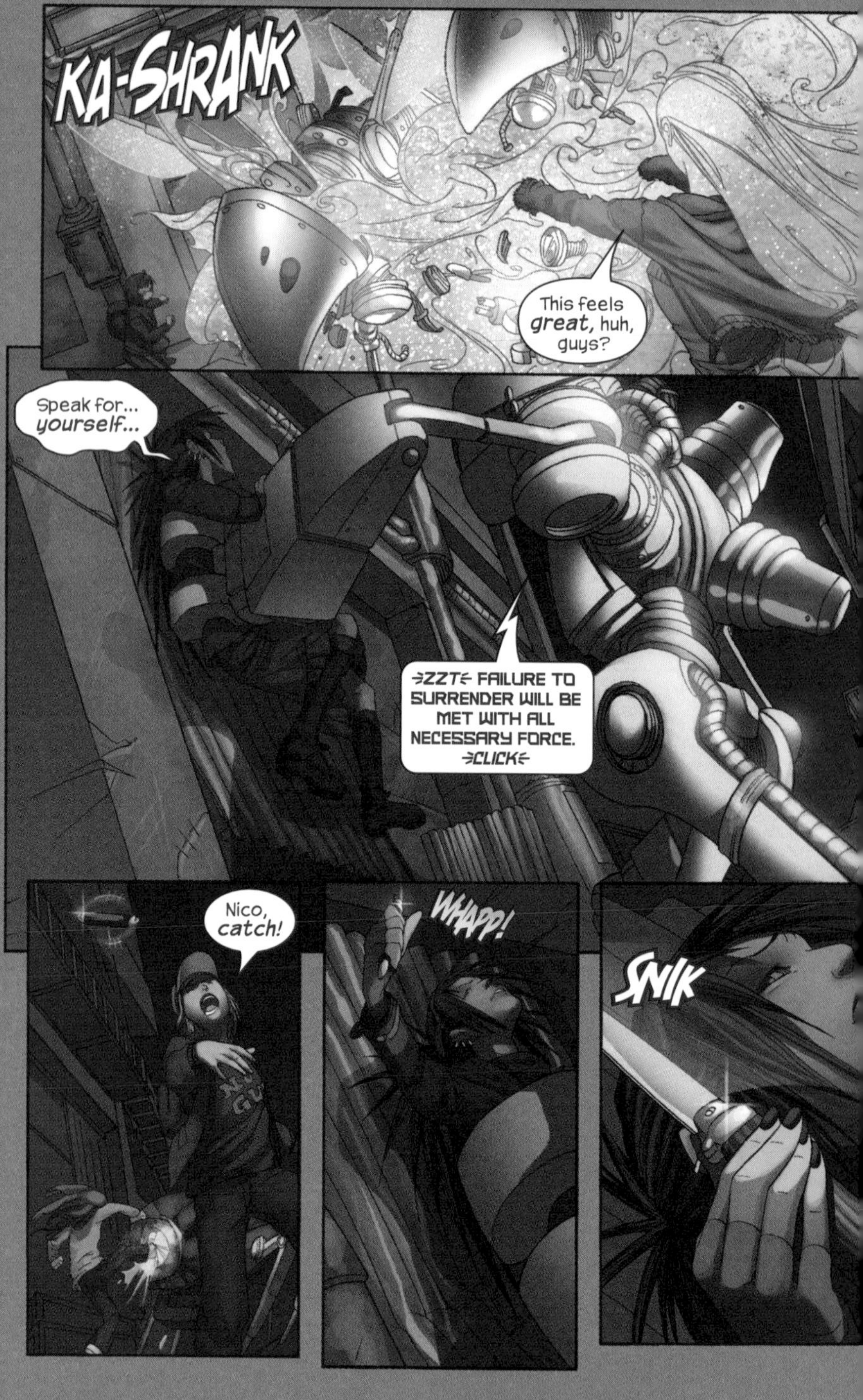
KA-SHRANK
This feels great, huh, guys?
Speak for... yourself...
ZZT FAILURE TO SURRENDER WILL BE MET WITH ALL NECESSARY FORCE. CLICK
Nico, catch!
WHAPP!
SNIK

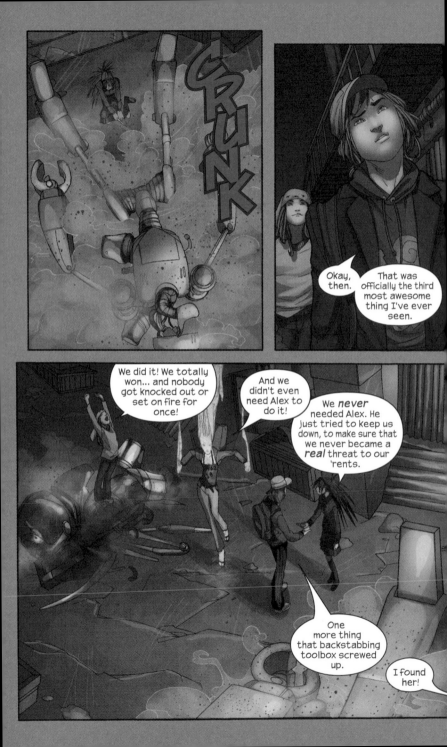

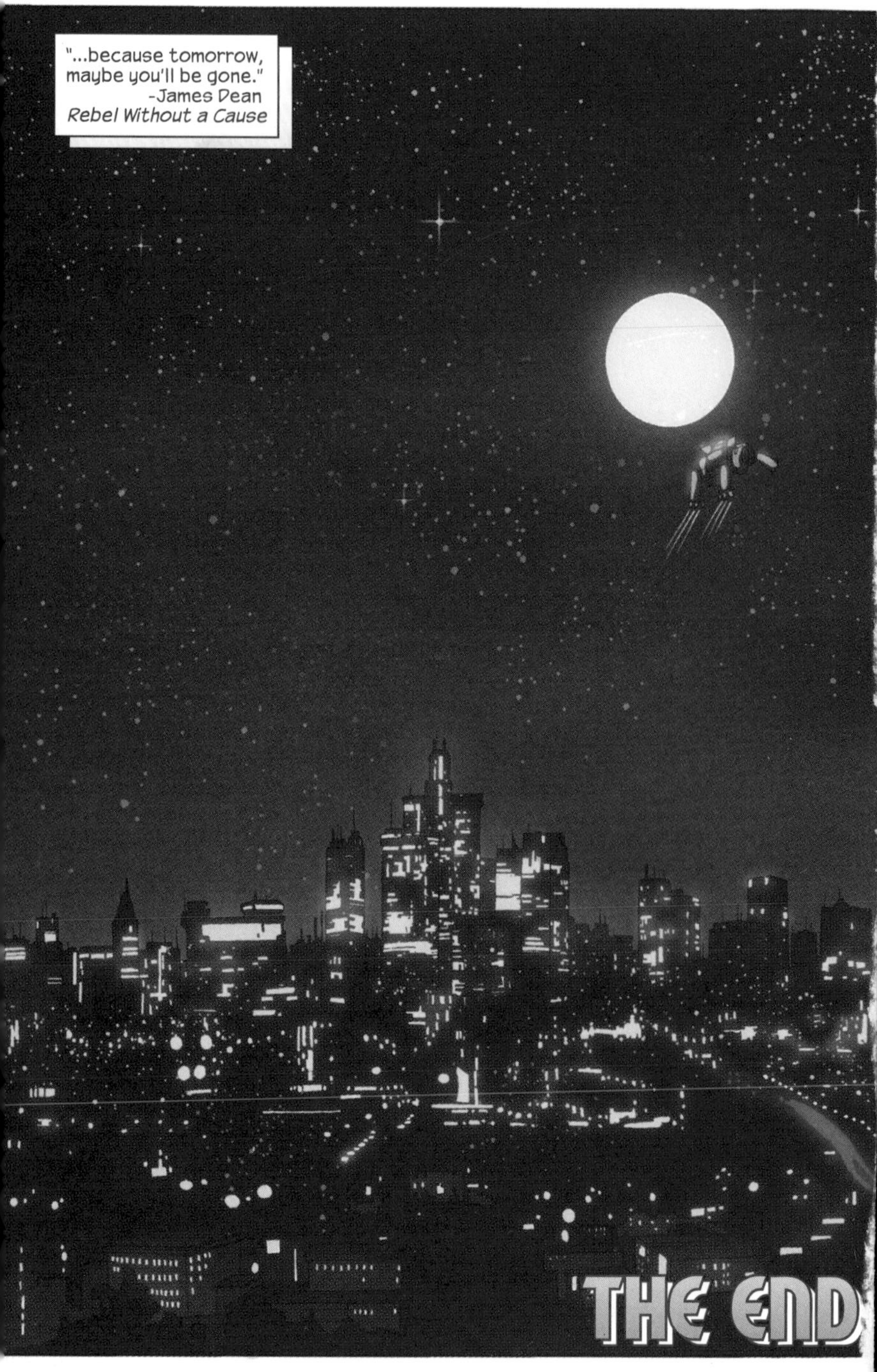
"...because tomorrow,
maybe you'll be gone."
-James Dean
Rebel Without a Cause
THE END